G000124208

Purple Ronnie's Star Signs

Virgo
23rd August - 22nd September

☆

First published 1994 by Statics (London) Ltd

This edition published 2002 by Boxtree
an imprint of Pan Macmillan Ltd
Pan Macmillan, 20 New Wharf Road, London N1 9RR
Basingstoke and Oxford
Associated companies throughout the world
www.panmacmillan.com

ISBN 0 7522 2046 2

A CIP catalogue record for this book is available from
the British Library

Text by Giles Andreae
Illustrations by Janet Cronin
Printed and bound in Hong Kong

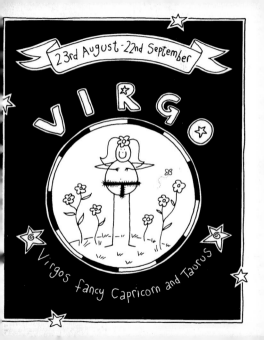

☆ Introduction ☆

Star Signs are a brilliant way of finding out about someone's character. You can use them to discover anything you like including what everyone's secretest rude fantasies are.

But reading what's written in the stars can only be done by incredibly brainy people like me. After gazing for ages through my gigantic telescope and doing loads of complicated sums and charts and stuff I have been able to work out exactly what everyone in the world is really like.

This book lets you know about all my amazing discoveries. It tells you what you look like, who your friends are, how your love life is, what you're like at Doing It and who you should be Doing It with.

Everything I've written in this book is completely true. Honest.

Love from

Purple Ronnie

xoX

Contents

Virgos are fussy and
boring
They like to be tidy
and neat
But the second they jump
At some rumpety-pump
They do it like hippos on
heat

✿ Virgo Looks ✿

Virgos are shy and quiet so you must not look at them for too long or they will go red and sweaty and start shuffling their feet

<u>Virgo Men</u>

Virgo Men have bulging tummies, specs and ginormous heads for fitting all their brains in

<u>Virgo Women</u>

Virgo Women have beautiful eyes, tidy hairstyles and boring clothes

comb   brush

✿ Virgo Character ✿

Virgos are incredibly brainy. They love facts and they often know all sorts of rubbish about everything

how many legs has a Mongolian millipede got?

BIG QUIZ

Virgos prefer reading books and having grown-up conversations to going to parties

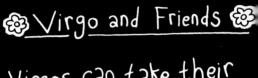 Virgo and Friends ✿

Virgos can take their
time to make friends
because they sometimes
seem snotty and rude
when all they are is shy

Virgos are kind and helpful...

...and good at looking
after their friends

GROWN-UP BUSINESS PEOPLE

because :-

1. They love working and are very interested in sums and computers

2. They like making lists and putting things in order

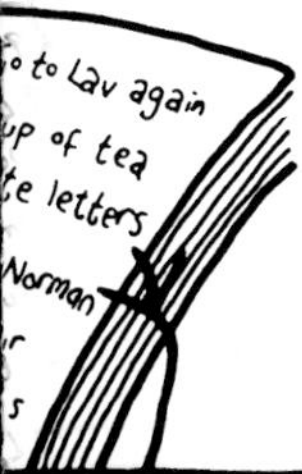

3. They are very sensible with money and love saving it up in little piles

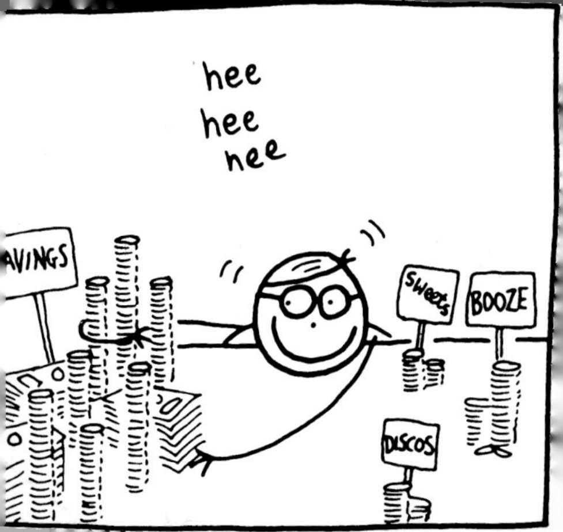
hee
hee
hee
AVINGS
Sweets
BOOZE
DISCOS

✿ Virgo and Love ✿

Virgos think falling in love is silly...

..and that there are more important things to be getting on with

Hmmm
BOY 1
not very handsome
nice car
funny ears
BOY 2
Big Nose
Too hairy
lots of money

Virgos choose their lovers with their heads and not their hearts

Warning:-

If your lover is a Virgo you will have to put up with lots of nagging and fussiness

where's my foot powder?... don't leave the lid off the toothpaste! ... have you got my botty cream?
rummage
shuffle

❀ Virgo and Sex ❀

Virgos can go for ages without having sex but once they find someone they fancy, they want to Do It with them till their bits drop off

Virgos like to do things properly so don't be surprised if they get out a book of instructions

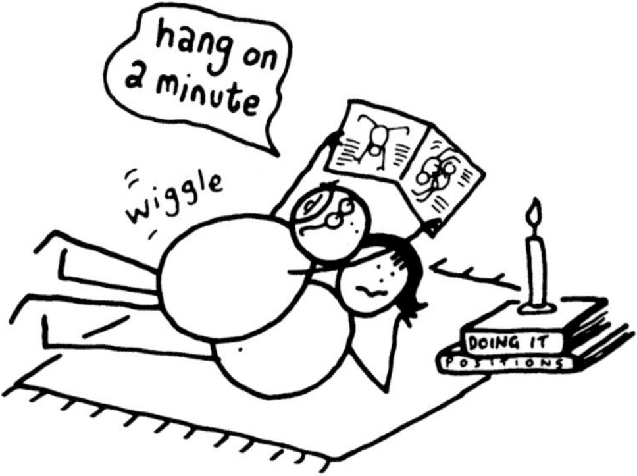
hang on
a minute
wiggle
DOING IT
POSITIONS

☆ Special Tip ☆

Most of all Virgos like
Doing It in the shower
because it's clean and
tidy and doesn't mess up
the bed

The End